THRIFTY COO

LIGHT MEALS & LUNCHBOXES

HOW TO MAKE A MONTH'S WORTH OF LUNCHES & LIGHT MEALS ON A BUDGET

Tessa Patterson

http://www.thriftycook.co.uk

Please look on my website for full colour photos of all the recipes

INTRODUCTION

It is one thing planning ahead and deciding what to cook for the daily main meal, but to plan ahead for everyone's lunch too can be difficult. People often get into the routine of buying a sandwich, yogurt, packet of crisps (chips) and a fizzy drink. The same goes for children's packed lunches ... Sandwiches can be boring day in and day out and expensive too, so why not spend a little time preparing the next day's lunch the night before? The recipes do not use specialist or expensive ingredients. Most of them are very quick and easy to make, some in as little as five minutes! All the recipes can be eaten cold and are ideal for picnics too.

The recipes can be halved or doubled depending on the number of servings. Some of the recipes use leftover food, for example, leftover roast chicken or cooked potatoes. There are also recipes that use a small amount of the same ingredient such as goats' cheese, which, even when opened to use in one recipe, will keep for a few days refrigerated until needed for another meal. When making the following recipes, do substitute any ingredients specific to your diet. For example, if you are vegetarian, use vegetarian rennet free cheese. Or if you are allergic to dairy produce, use soya milk instead.

I like to use lots of herbs when cooking. Rather than buying pre-packed herbs, have a go at growing them on the kitchen windowsill. This works out much cheaper than buying them packaged and the herbs will be completely fresh.

Make sure that any cooked meal is cooled completely, covered and stored in the refrigerator.

Wash vegetables, salad and fruit thoroughly before preparing them. Salads, in particular, need drying carefully before using especially if they are stored for several hours in the refrigerator.

Always prepare uncooked meat on a separate chopping board to other ingredients. I use two boards, one for meat and fish and the other for slicing vegetables, carving bread and so on.

Above all, enjoy preparing and eating the recipes!

CONTENTS

CHEESE PIE	36
CHICKPEA AND BEETROOT DIP	37
CHICKEN COUSCOUS SALAD	38
CHICKEN, PEANUT AND LIME SALAD	39
CHEESE AND HAM SLICES	40
SARDINE PÂTÉ	42

NOTES

LITTLE CHEESE AND CHIVE PIES

Vegetarian

Oven

Serves 4 – makes 12 small pies

Preparation 15 minutes/Cook 15-20 minutes

Preheat oven to 190C/Fan 170/375F/Gas 5

Delicious eaten warm or cold. This quantity will serve 4 people (3 pies each)

1lb/400g shortcrust pastry
1oz/25g Parmesan cheese grated
8oz/250g Mascarpone cheese
1 egg
1 tbsp snipped chives
Black pepper

You'll need a 12 bun muffin tin or similar.

Roll out the pastry thinly and using a 4"/10cm cutter or any other circular guide (e.g. a large mug), cut out 12 circles (re-rolling the pastry to use the off cuts). Lay the pastry rounds over the tins and press down gently so that the pastry fits the base and sides of the tins.

Beat the mascarpone, egg, snipped chives and black pepper in a bowl. Divide the cheese mixture between the pie cases. Sprinkle the Parmesan cheese over the top of each pie. Place in the oven and bake for about 15-20 minutes until golden.

Leave to cool and set a little if eating warm.

CHICKEN & NECTARINE SALAD

No Cooking

Serves 4

Preparation 10 minutes

A very simple, tasty salad using leftover chicken.

10oz/300g/2 cups of leftover cooked chicken
2 ripe nectarines
1 crispy lettuce such as Little Gem, Cos or Iceberg
4 tbsp oil (olive oil or canola for example)
1 tsp Dijon or wholegrain mustard
1 tsp honey
1 tbsp fresh or 1 tsp dried tarragon
Black pepper

Wash, dry and slice the lettuce and put in a bowl. Tear or chop the chicken into chunks and add to the bowl. Wash and slice the nectarines and scatter over the chicken.

To make the dressing, combine the oil, mustard, honey, tarragon and a little black pepper. Mix well then pour over the salad.

CHEESY MUSHROOM PIES

Vegetarian

Oven

Serves 1

Preparation 10 minutes/Cook 15-20 minutes

Preheat oven to 190C/Fan 170/375F/Gas 5

Delicious mushroom pies. Good hot or cold. If you want to serve two people, double the recipe, or for four – quadruple and so on. You can buy cream cheese with garlic and herbs in a tub, so use that by all means if you'd like to.

1 large flat mushroom
1 garlic clove crushed
1 tbsp cream cheese
6oz/175g puff pastry (I use bought)
1 egg beaten
A pinch of dried herbs

Roll out the pastry to approx 12" x 6" (30cm x 15cm). Take the stem off the mushroom. Imagine the pastry divided in half, place the mushroom on the centre of one half of the pastry, base side down.

Put the cream cheese, garlic and herbs in the cavity of the mushroom.

Brush a little egg onto the outer edges of the pastry then fold the pastry over the mushroom. Enclose the mushroom completely and press the pastry down around all sides. Make a couple of slits on the top of the pastry with a sharp knife to let the steam escape when cooking. Trim the edges if needed. Place on a baking sheet.

Brush the top and sides with the remaining beaten egg. Cook for about 15-20 minutes until the pastry is risen and golden.

Serve hot or cold with a rocket or other green salad. Delicious!

BEETROOT, WALNUT AND GOATS' CHEESE SALAD

Vegetarian

No Cooking

Serves 1

Preparation 5 minutes

A very easy, tasty salad. Glamorous enough to entertain friends at lunchtime!

1 cooked beetroot (not pickled)
2 oz/50g walnuts or pecan nuts
2 oz/50g goats' cheese
A bunch of watercress or crunchy lettuce leaves
2 tbsp olive oil
1 tbsp balsamic vinegar (or your favourite vinegar)

Dice the beetroot. Roughly chop the nuts. Slice or cube the cheese. Put the beetroot, nuts and cheese in a bowl and mix together. Pile the watercress or lettuce leaves on a plate. Spoon over the beetroot, cheese and nut mixture then drizzle with the oil and vinegar.

HAM AND SWEETCORN PASTA SALAD

Hob (broiler)

Serves 4

Preparation 5 minutes/Cook 10 minutes

So easy to make and brilliant for a packed lunch.

4oz/100g/ ½ cup cooked ham or cooked cold sausage - diced
8oz/200g/1 cup pasta – whatever you have. I use spiral shaped pasta
8oz/200g/1 cup frozen sweetcorn kernels
2 sticks of celery
3 rounded tbsp mayonnaise
Parsley (optional)
Black pepper

Cook the pasta in boiling water according to instructions on pack. When cooked, drain and add the sweetcorn. Allow to cool and then add the ham. Slice the celery and add to the pasta bowl along with the mayonnaise, chopped parsley and black pepper. Mix well.

EGG AND VEGETABLE SALAD

Vegetarian

Hob (broiler)

Serves 2

Preparation 10 minutes/Cook 10 minutes

An egg salad made with peas, sweetcorn and gherkins.

4 eggs
4oz/100g/ ¾ cup peas (fresh or frozen)
40z/100g/ ¾ cup sweetcorn (frozen)
4 tbsp mayonnaise
Small bunch of chives – or you could use spring onions (scallions)
4 small pickled gherkins (or cucumber)

Hard boil the eggs: half fill a saucepan with boiling water, put the eggs in and simmer on medium heat for about 8 minutes.

When cooked, drain the water and fill the saucepan up with cold water. Set aside for the eggs to cool.

Boil the peas and sweetcorn for about 2 minutes then drain really well.

Chop the gherkins into small pieces.

Peel the eggs and put in a mixing bowl. Mash them up gently with a fork. Add the drained peas, sweetcorn, mayonnaise and gherkins. Snip the chives over with scissors. Season with black pepper. Mix well.

Serve with bread or melba toast.

CHEESE AND TOMATO TORTILLA

Vegetarian

Oven

Serves 6-8

Preparation 15 minutes/Cook 30 minutes

Preheat oven to 190C/Fan 170/375F/Gas 5

This tortilla can be eaten warm or cold. I like to make this large one as it always gets eaten for lunch within a couple of days! For two people, why not have most of this in the evening and keep the rest for lunch? Or, you can easily halve the ingredients to make a light meal for 3-4 people.

1lb/500g/2 cups baby potatoes boiled
4oz/100g/1 cup Cheddar cheese
4 eggs
2 Medium sized tomatoes sliced
2 ½ fl oz/50ml/ ¼ cup milk
2 garlic cloves
2 tbsp chopped chives
Black pepper

You will need an ovenproof dish measuring approx 12"x 6" (30cm x 15cm).

Slice the potatoes into chunks and spread around in the dish.

Crack the eggs into a bowl and add the cheese, chives, pepper, garlic and milk. Mix.

Pour the eggy mixture over the potatoes. Arrange the slices of tomatoes over the top.

Bake for about 30 minutes until lightly golden. Leave to cool a little before serving.

EASY CORONATION CHICKEN

No cooking

Serves 2

Preparation 5 minutes

A very quick and easy way to make the classic Coronation Chicken dish using very basic ingredients and leftover chicken.

8oz/200g/1 cup cooked chicken (breast or thigh)
1 spring onion (scallion)
½ - 1 tsp curry powder
1 tbsp mango chutney
3 tbsp mayonnaise
1oz/30g sultanas
Pinch of salt and black pepper
Crispy lettuce leaves to serve

Soak the sultanas in a small bowl or cup of boiling water.

Wash and slice the spring onions (scallions) thinly.

Mix the mayonnaise, mango chutney, curry powder and spring onions in a bowl. Chop or tear the chicken and add that to the mayonnaise mixture. Drain the sultanas well and mix them in.

Rather than serving alone, this chicken recipe is fantastic served in crunchy lettuce leaves. Wash and dry the leaves, put a dollop of the chicken mixture on each leaf then roll up. Secure with a cocktail stick if needed.

TOMATO AND CHORIZO TARTS

Oven

Serves 4

Preparation 10 minutes/Cook 20 minutes

Preheat oven to 200C/Fan 180/400F/Gas 6

I have made these tarts using filo and short pastry but find that puff pastry works best. The recipe only uses a small amount of chorizo but there are other recipes in this book where you can use up the rest of the sausage. Or, buy a small quantity ready sliced. By all means, use another type of sausage if you have a favourite.

4 medium or about 12 cherry tomatoes
1oz/30g chorizo sausage (skin taken off)
4oz/100g mozzarella cheese grated
½ lb/250g readymade puff pastry
2 spring onions (scallions)
½ tbsp oil

Grease 4 ramekins or bun tins (measuring approx. 4"/10cm diameter).

Wash and dice the spring onions (scallions), wash and quarter the tomatoes. Slice the chorizo into fairly small pieces.

Roll out the pastry and, using a template, for example an upturned saucer or small plate, cut the pastry into 4 rounds slightly larger than the ramekins or bun tins. Place each round in the tin, pressing down gently. Leave the overlapping pastry as this will be used to enclose the tarts later.

Place a quarter of the spring onions in the base of each tart. Top with the sliced chorizo. Add some mozzarella and finally, the tomatoes.

Fold over the excess pastry towards the centre of the tarts, it won't completely cover them but will make them easier to eat cold. Brush the pastry with a little oil. Bake for about 20 minutes until the pastry has puffed up and is slightly golden.

FETA AND BEAN SALAD

Vegetarian

No cooking

Serves 2

Preparation 5 minutes

A very quick and tasty dish. I haven't added salt as feta cheese tends to be quite salty.

8oz/230g can red kidney beans drained
80z/230g can cannellini beans drained
4oz/100g feta cheese
2 sticks celery
2 tbsp parsley
3 tbsp olive or canola oil
2 tbsp white vinegar
1 clove garlic
Black pepper

Place the drained beans into a mixing bowl. Chop the feta cheese into cubes. Slice the celery finely. Chop the parsley. Peel and crush the garlic clove. Add all the above ingredients to the beans.

Add the oil, vinegar and season with black pepper. Mix well.

CHICKEN & WALNUT WRAPS

No cooking

Serves 2

Preparation 10 minutes

If you like plenty of "crunch" in a wrap then don't chop the celery or walnuts too finely. This recipe is quick to make, delicious and uses leftover chicken. If you would like to make your own Chinese plum sauce, then have a look on my website for a very easy recipe!

8oz/200g/1 cup cooked chicken
2oz/50g walnuts
2 celery sticks
A few crunchy lettuce leaves e.g. Little Gem, Cos or Iceberg
3 tbsp mayonnaise
1-2 tbsp mint leaves
4 tbsp Chinese plum sauce (optional, or mild chilli sauce)
Black pepper
4 soft tortilla wraps (homemade or bought)

Shred or tear the chicken into fairly small pieces. Chop the walnuts. Slice the celery. Finely chop the mint. Put all the above ingredients into a mixing bowl. Add the mayonnaise and season with black pepper. Mix.

Lay out one of the wraps and spread 1 tbsp plum sauce over. Add a quarter of the chicken and walnut mixture and top with some lettuce leaves. Roll up tightly. Repeat with the other 3 wraps.

If preparing these wraps for the next day, wrap each one up tightly in plastic film and twist each end to seal so that they keep their shape.

AWESOME SAUSAGE ROLLS

Oven

Serves 4 – makes 8 sausage rolls

Preparation 15 minutes/Cook 20-25 minutes

Preheat oven to 200C/Fan 180/400F/Gas 6

Delicious served warm or cold.

1lb/500g readymade puff pastry
8 sausages
1 small red onion
1 carrot
1 small courgette (zucchini)
1 tsp sage
Salt and black pepper
1 egg beaten

Grate or finely slice the onion, carrot and courgette (zucchini). Squeeze excess juice from the courgette. Add all to a mixing bowl together with the sage.

Snip the end off each sausage and squeeze the meat out into the bowl, discarding the skins. Add a little salt and black pepper. Mix thoroughly.

On a lightly floured surface, roll out the pastry into a rectangle measuring approx. 15"x 8"/38x20cm. Cut down the middle to form 2 long rectangles. Place half of the filling evenly down the centre of one piece of pastry. Repeat with the other piece.

Brush a little egg on the outer edges of the pastry and roll up to form a long "sausage" shape. Brush the remaining egg on the top and sides.

Cut each into 4 sausage rolls. With a sharp knife, make a couple of slashes on the top of each sausage roll.

Carefully spread out onto a baking sheet, overlapping side down, and cook for about 20-25 minutes until golden.

COUSCOUS WITH GOATS' CHEESE & WALNUT PESTO

Vegetarian

No cooking

Serves 2

Preparation 10 minutes

Quick to make, filling and delicious!

6oz/190g/1 cup couscous
¼ pint/120ml/ ½ cup boiling water
4 sundried or fresh tomatoes
4 tbsp oil (if using sundried then use the oil from the jar for more flavour)
2 oz/50g walnuts
2 oz/50g goats' cheese
Large handful of mint leaves
Salt and black pepper

Place the dry couscous in a mixing bowl and add the hot water, mix gently then leave to one side whilst preparing the other ingredients.

Chop the tomatoes. Pulse the walnuts, mint leaves and oil in a food processor a few times until the mixture is chopped and combined but not completely smooth. If you don't have a processor, finely chop the walnuts and mint, put into a small bowl and mix in the oil.

Mix the couscous with a fork until all the water is absorbed. Chop the cheese into bite sized pieces and add to the couscous. Add the tomatoes. Pour the walnut and mint mixture over. Add some black pepper.

Mix well before serving.

SPICY CHICKEN PIECES WITH TOMATOES AND HERBS

Oven and hob (broiler)

Serves 2

Preparation 15 minutes/Cook 45-60 minutes

Preheat oven to 180C/Fan 160/350F/Gas 4

These tasty, spicy chicken pieces are perfect hot for lunch or cold for packed lunches or picnics.

6-8 chicken pieces (wings, thighs or drumsticks)
2 cloves garlic minced
1 tsp ground cumin
1 tsp paprika
5fl oz/150ml/ ½ cup oil
3 tomatoes
Handful of basil leaves
Salt and black pepper

Mix 2 tbsp oil in a fairly large bowl with the cumin, paprika and garlic.
Put the chicken pieces in the bowl and rub the spicy dressing in well. Then wash your hands well!

Put 2 tbsp oil in a frying pan (skillet) and fry the chicken portions on both sides (about 15 minutes) until browned.

Transfer the chicken to a roasting tin and put in the oven for about 30 minutes, turning half way through cooking.

Meanwhile, chop the tomatoes into small pieces and put in a bowl. Add the rest of the oil. Season with salt and pepper.

When the chicken is cooked (the juices should run clear when putting a sharp knife in the middle part of the chicken), put in a serving bowl. Pour the tomato dressing over the cooked chicken and cover with kitchen film. Leave to cool. Tear the leaves off the basil (I like to use Greek basil because of its pungent flavour) and scatter over the dish before serving.

ASPARAGUS & CHORIZO TORTILLA

Oven

Serves 4-6

Preparation 10 minutes/Cook 30-35 minutes

Preheat oven to 180C/Fan 160/350F/Gas 4

If asparagus is not in season you could substitute it with purple sprouting broccoli or calabrese. Use leftover potatoes if you have any. This dish is good warm or cold.

Small bunch of asparagus
4oz/100g chorizo sausage
1lb/500g boiled potatoes
6 eggs
¼ pint/150ml/ ½ cup of milk or cream
1 tbsp thyme leaves (optional) or other herb you have e.g. basil or mint
Black pepper

Grease a 12" x 8"/30cm x 20cm ovenproof dish (rectangular makes the tortilla easier to slice).

Snap the woody ends off the asparagus, wash it then boil gently for 2-3 minutes. When cooked, drain well and set to one side.

Slice the potatoes into chunks. Slice the chorizo into bite sized pieces.

In a bowl, beat the eggs and milk or cream. Season and add the thyme leaves. Place the chorizo around the base of the dish, spread the potatoes and asparagus over the chorizo. Pour the beaten egg mixture over the top.

Bake until lightly golden.

N.B. If you have to cook the potatoes rather than using leftovers, boil in lightly salted water for 15-20 minutes with a lid on. When cooked, remove with a slotted spoon and cook the asparagus for 2-3 minutes in the same water.

BLUE CHEESE AND WALNUT PÂTÉ

Vegetarian

No cooking

Serves 2

Preparation 10 minutes

This dish needs making in advance so that it can be refrigerated for a few hours before eating. Try to use a fairly mild blue cheese.

8oz/200g/1 ¾ cups mild blue cheese with creamy texture
4oz/100g/ ½ cup cream cheese
1 stick celery
A small handful of walnuts
1 spring onion (scallion)
Black pepper

Crumble up the blue cheese and put in a mixing bowl. Add the cream cheese. Chop the cucumber and spring onion (scallion) very finely and add to the bowl together with some black pepper. Mix everything well.

Chop the walnuts into small pieces, or bang them with a rolling pin on a wooden board. You need them to look a little bigger than breadcrumbs.

Take a rectangular piece of greaseproof paper and put the cheese mixture down the centre so that the length of the mixture is about 6"/15cm. Lift the sides of the paper up and over the cheese then roll into a sausage shape.

Spread the walnuts evenly over a chopping board. Unwrap the cheese and roll over the walnuts so that the sides of the cheese are covered in walnuts. Wrap the cheese up again in the paper and twist the ends (a bit like a cracker). Put in the refrigerator to set.

To serve, simply slice and serve with salad.

TUNA SALAD

Vegetarian

Hob (broiler)

Serves 2

Preparation 10 minutes/Cook 5 minutes

A tasty salad made with tuna, sweetcorn and cucumber. Great for packed lunches and picnics.

6oz/160g can tuna chunks well drained
4oz/100g frozen or canned sweetcorn
¼ cucumber
1 lemon
4 tbsp mayonnaise
6 cherry tomatoes
½ tsp Dijon mustard (optional)
Black pepper

Put the drained tuna in a bowl.

Simmer the sweetcorn for about 3-5 minutes then drain really well. Dice or grate the cucumber then squeeze out the juice. Add the cucumber to the bowl. Quarter the tomatoes and add to the bowl.

Place the mayonnaise, mustard, juice from the lemon and black pepper (to taste) in a small bowl and mix.

Pour the dressing over the tuna mixture.

Serve with crusty bread.

RICE WITH BLACK BEANS

Vegetarian

Hob (broiler)

Serves 2
Preparation 10 minutes/Cook 12 minutes

A dish made with rice, black beans, and red bell peppers. The recipe is based on Spanish rice dishes where beans and spices are often combined to make delicious salads.

4oz/100g/ ½ cup white long grain rice
12oz/380g carton black beans in water
2 spring onions (scallions)
1 red bell pepper
Chicken or vegetable stock (see below)
1 tsp ground cinnamon
1 lime
Salt and black pepper

Cook the rice according to the instructions on the pack but substitute the water for stock (either fresh or instant).

When cooked, drain well. Put into a serving dish.

Slice the spring onions (scallions), de-seed and finely chop the red pepper, drain the black beans. Add these ingredients to the bowl together with salt, pepper, cinnamon and squeezed lime juice. Stir well.

CHICKEN AND RED PEPPER PASTIES

Oven

Serves 4 – makes 4 pasties

Preparation 15 minutes/Cook 20-25 minutes

Preheat oven to 200C/Fan 180/400F/Gas 6

Pasties with chicken, red bell pepper and basil.

1lb/500g readymade puff pastry
12 oz/350g/ 1 ½ cups cooked chicken
1 large red bell pepper
½ - 1 tsp dried chilli flakes, chilli powder or small red chilli diced
1 garlic clove
1 egg beaten
Large handful of fresh basil leaves

Chop the red bell pepper into small pieces and place in a mixing bowl. Chop or tear the chicken into bite size pieces and add to the bowl. Crush the garlic and add to the bowl together with the chilli and basil leaves. Mix well.

Roll out the pastry fairly thinly and cut into 4 circles measuring about 7"/18cm diameter. Place quarter of the chicken mixture on one half of each pastry circle, leaving a ¼"/1.3cm gap around the edge.

Brush a little beaten egg around the edges of the pastry. Fold the pastry over to make a pasty shape. Seal the edges by gently pressing down. Crimp the edges with a fork then brush the pasties with the remaining egg. Make a small slit in the top of each pasty to allow the steam to escape.

Bake until golden.

FANCY POTATO SALAD

Vegetarian

Hob (broiler)

Serves 2

Preparation 10 minutes/Cook 8 minutes

A very simple salad using leftover potatoes.

1 lb/500g/2 ½ cups cooked new potatoes halved
8 cherry tomatoes or 3 medium tomatoes
2 eggs
1 spring onion (scallion)
2-3 tbsp mayonnaise
2-3 tbsp parsley
Black pepper or paprika

For extra flavour, add either some flaked tuna, sliced anchovies, diced cucumber, ham, peas or sweetcorn.

Place the eggs in a saucepan of boiling water and simmer for about 8 minutes. Whilst the eggs are cooking, quarter the tomatoes, finely slice the spring onion (scallion) and chop the parsley then place them all in a mixing bowl.

When the eggs are cooked, tap each egg to break the shell then peel carefully under running water. Set aside to cool for a few minutes. When cool, slice into quarters.

Add the eggs to the bowl together with the mayonnaise. Season with black pepper or a couple of pinches of paprika. Mix.

HERBY COUSCOUS WITH FETA & TOMATOES

Vegetarian

No cooking

Serves 2

Preparation 10 minutes

Quick to make and this dish has beautiful summery flavours. You don't need to add salt as feta cheese is salty enough.

8oz/200g/1 cup couscous
4oz/100g/ ½ cup Feta cheese
8 cherry tomatoes
4tbs oil
Large handful of mint leaves
Pinch of oregano
½ small cucumber
½ pint/250ml/1 cup boiling water
Black pepper

Place the dry couscous in a bowl and cover with the boiling water. Use a fork to stir and break up the pieces. Leave to one side to cool.

Slice the tomatoes into quarters. Chop the cucumber into small chunks. Cut the feta into bite sized pieces. Chop the herbs finely.

Put all the above into the bowl of couscous and add the oil and black pepper. Mix well.

PORK AND CHEESE PIE

Oven and hob (broiler)

Serves 4-6

Preparation 20 minutes/Cook 30-40 minutes

Preheat oven to 180C/Fan 160/350F/Gas 4

This pie can be served warm or cold. Perfect for lunchboxes or picnics.

6oz/170g shortcrust pastry
1lb/500g/2 cups minced pork
2-3 spring onions (scallions)
2 cloves garlic
2 eggs
3oz/85g/¾ cup cheese (e.g. cheddar) grated
2 tbsp oil for frying
1 tsp milk
Salt and black pepper

You will need a greased pie dish (square or rectangular is best) measuring about
6" x 6"/15 x15cm.

Set aside one third of the pastry for the lid. Roll out the remaining pastry so that it
covers the base and sides of the dish allowing about 1"/2.5cm overhang.
Carefully place into the dish, leaving the excess to hang over the sides.

Crush the garlic cloves and finely slice the spring onions (scallions). Put the oil into
a frying pan (skillet) on medium heat and fry the garlic for about a minute, stirring.

Add the minced pork and using a spoon, break the meat up. Continue stirring
the pork for about 5 minutes. Put the pork and garlic into a mixing bowl.

Add the spring onions, cheese, eggs, black pepper and a little salt. Mix well then
spoon into the pie case. Press down gently with a spatula to level the top.

Roll out the remaining pastry to make a lid. Place the pastry on top of the pork
mixture. Fold the overhanging sides over the top of the pie lid and press down
with the tines of a fork.

Brush the pie with milk then stab a few holes in the top with the fork.

Bake for about 30-40 minutes until the pastry is a light golden colour.

CHICKEN PASTA SALAD

Hob (broiler)

Serves 2

Preparation 10 minutes/Cook 5-10 minutes plus allow time for the pasta to cool.

A tasty salad with lots of texture and flavour. You could use ham instead of chicken or to make a vegetarian version, leave out the meat and add a few more walnuts.

8oz/200g/2 cups small pasta shapes or macaroni
4oz/100g/1 cup cooked, diced chicken
2 celery sticks
2oz/50g/ $1/3$ cup frozen peas
2oz/50g/ $1/3$ cup frozen sweetcorn kernels
2 tbsp walnuts
4 tbsp mayonnaise
Handful of parsley or tarragon

Cook the pasta in salted boiling water according to the instructions on the pack. This will usually take between 5 and 10 minutes depending on the size of the pasta shapes.

Whilst the pasta is cooking, slice the celery and chop the herbs finely. Roughly chop the walnuts.

When the pasta is cooked, add the peas and sweetcorn to the pan, stir, then drain everything in a colander. The heat from the pasta will defrost the vegetables. Rinse the colander under cold water to cool the pasta and vegetables. Drain well and put in a mixing bowl.

Add the celery, walnuts, mayonnaise and herbs.

When the pasta is cold, add the chicken. Mix well.

CHORIZO AND RED PEPPER SALAD

Hob (broiler)

Serves 2

Preparation 5 minutes/Cook 15-20 minutes (If using uncooked potatoes)

A simple but delicious salad. Use leftover potatoes if you have them. If you have any leftovers from this dish, add a little oil to a frying pan (skillet), add the chorizo and potato mixture, cook for a few minutes, stirring until heated through. Then crack in 2 eggs, stir and cook through to make a tasty omelette.

½ chorizo sausage – outer skin removed (or any other spicy sausage)
1lb/500g of cooked new potatoes
3 spring onions (scallions)
1 clove garlic
1 red bell pepper – either fresh or from a jar
2 tbsp parsley (or any other herb you have e.g. basil or thyme)
1 tbsp oil

Cut the potatoes in half and put in a mixing bowl. Trim the spring onions (scallions) and chop finely. Remove the stem and seeds from the red pepper then chop into small pieces. Slice the chorizo thinly. Crush the garlic.

Put the oil in a frying pan (skillet) and fry the chorizo for a minute or two on each side on medium heat. Add the spring onions, garlic and red pepper. Stir and cook for a couple of minutes until everything has softened.

Pour the chorizo mixture onto the potatoes. Add the herbs and stir well.

LEEK, COURGETTE & TOMATO TIAN

Vegetarian

Oven and hob (broiler)

Serves 4-6

Preparation 20 minutes/Cook 30-40 minutes
Preheat oven to 180C/Fan 160/350F/Gas 4

This dish is similar to a quiche but without the pastry. Layers of vegetables, herbs, eggs and milk. As the filling is fairly soft, it will need to be eaten with a fork. By all means, halve the quantities for 2-3 people and use 2 eggs.

1 large leek
2 medium courgettes (zucchini)
3 medium or 2 large tomatoes
2 tbsp/1oz/30g butter
2 tbsp flour
½ pint/300ml/1 cup milk
3 eggs
Handful of fresh mint leaves
Salt and black pepper

Grease a 12" x 8"/30cm x 20cm ovenproof dish.

Slice the leeks thinly then wash thoroughly to get rid of soil and grit. Drain well.

Slice the courgettes (zucchini) very finely. Slice the tomatoes. Chop the mint.

Melt the butter in a saucepan over medium heat and stir in the leeks. Simmer for about 5 minutes stirring occasionally. Stir in the flour and gradually stir in the milk. Keep stirring for about 5 minutes until thickened a little. Take the saucepan off the heat and mix in the eggs. Add salt and pepper.

Put the leek mixture in the base of the baking dish and scatter over the mint.

Place slices of courgette evenly over the top. Finish with a layer of sliced tomatoes.

Bake in the centre of the oven for about 25-30 minutes. Check that the courgettes are soft and if not, cover the dish with a piece of foil and return to the oven for another 10 minutes.

Leave to cool a little before serving.

CHEESE PIE

Vegetarian

Oven

Serves 4-6

Preparation 10 minutes/Cook 30 minutes
Preheat oven to 180C/Fan 160/350F/Gas 4

An easy pie to make and it tastes really good warm or cold. Try to buy good quality cottage cheese. If it is full of liquid then drain first.

8oz/200g shortcrust pastry
8oz/200g/¾ cup feta cheese cubed
10oz/300g/1 ¹/₃ cups cottage cheese
2 tbsp cornflour (cornstarch)
1 tsp baking powder
¼ pint/150ml/½ cup milk
2 eggs beaten

Grease and line a 9"/22cm round baking tin.

Mix the cheeses, cornflour (cornstarch), baking powder and milk in a bowl. Put a small amount of egg (about 2 tsp) in a separate bowl (this will be used to brush over the pie before cooking). Add the rest of the beaten egg to the cheese mixture. Stir everything well.

Roll out the pastry to approx 14"/35cm (which will be bigger than the baking tin). Place the pastry on the baking tin and press gently so that the pastry covers the base and sides. There will surplus pastry around the edges.

Spoon the cheesy filling into the baking tin, smooth the top to make the filling even. Fold over the surplus pastry to the inside of the pie, pinching it to fit (It doesn't need to be perfect!) Brush the reserved egg over the top of the pastry.

Bake for about 30 minutes until golden. Take out of the oven and leave to cool for about 30 minutes before serving.

CHICKPEA AND BEETROOT DIP

Vegetarian

No cooking

Serves 2

Preparation 5 minutes

Very easy and quick to make. Leave out the cumin if you don't want a spicy flavour.

8oz/200g can chickpeas drained
4oz/100g/ ¾ cup cooked beetroot (not pickled)
4oz/100g/ ½ cup cream cheese
1 clove garlic
¼ - ½ tsp dried cumin
Pinch of salt

Place the chickpeas in a bowl. Chop the beetroot into small chunks and add to the chickpeas. Add the cream cheese, cumin and salt. Crush the garlic clove and add that too.

Stir and crush everything in the bowl with a fork until well mixed, or pulse for a few seconds in a food processor.

Serve with breadsticks, pitta bread, flatbreads, naan bread or vegetable sticks (e.g. celery, cucumber or carrot).

CHICKEN COUSCOUS SALAD

No cooking

Serves 4

Preparation 10 minutes

A dish using up chicken leftovers. Tasty and filling. Great for lunch, picnic or lunchbox.

8oz/200g/1 cup couscous
8oz/200g/2 cups cooked chicken
8-12 cherry tomatoes
Large handful of basil leaves
1 large lemon
3 tbsp olive or canola oil
½ pint/300ml/1 cup boiling water
Salt and black pepper

Place the couscous in a bowl and add the boiling water. Mix well with a fork. Squeeze the lemon juice over the couscous and add the oil. Stir.

Quarter the tomatoes, tear up the basil leaves and add to the bowl. Chop or tear the chicken into bite sized pieces. Add the chicken to the bowl together with some salt and pepper to taste. Stir.

CHICKEN, PEANUT AND LIME SALAD

Hob (broiler)

Serves 2

Preparation 10 minutes/Cook 5-10 minutes

A delicious crunchy salad made with leftover chicken and stale bread.

4 thick slices of stale bread
8oz/200g/2 cups cooked chicken
1 rounded tbsp peanut butter
Juice of 1 large lime
A crispy lettuce e.g. Cos, Little Gem or Iceberg
2 tbsp butter
2 tbsp oil
1 tbsp mayonnaise
A pinch of garlic salt or a minced garlic clove
Black pepper

Cut the bread into ¾"/2cm cubes. Melt the butter and oil in a frying pan (skillet) on medium to low heat and place the cubes of bread in it. Sprinkle the garlic salt or minced garlic over. Shake the pan gently and check whether the bread is browning underneath. Keep the heat low so that the garlic and bread don't burn. When the bread has browned, turn over to cook the other side. Place the cooked croutons on kitchen paper to drain.

Put the peanut butter, lime juice, mayonnaise and some black pepper in a mixing bowl. Beat well until smooth. Add the cooked chicken and stir in.

Tear the lettuce up and divide between two plates (or lunchboxes). Divide the chicken mixture and spoon over the lettuce. Scatter the croutons on top.

CHEESE AND HAM SLICES

Oven and hob (broiler)

Serves 4

Preparation 15 minutes/Cook 20-25 minutes
Preheat oven to 200C/Fan 180/425F/Gas 7

Slices made with puff pastry, cheese and ham ends (also known as bacon misshapes, bacon ends, bacon lardons). These are very cheap to buy and taste good.

4oz/100g/ ½ cup cooked potato
1lb/500g readymade puff pastry
1lb/500g ham ends (bacon misshapes or lardons)
2oz/50g cheese grated
2 tbsp flour
1 tbsp oil
5 fl oz/100ml/ ½ cup milk
1 tbsp parsley
1 egg beaten
Black pepper

Chop the fat off the ham ends and discard.

Put the oil in a frying pan (skillet) and fry the ham ends on medium to high heat for about 5 minutes, stirring every now and then. Turn the heat down, stir in the flour and gradually add the milk stirring constantly.

Add the grated cheese, parsley and black pepper. Stir until the sauce is smooth. Take off the heat and set to one side to cool a little.

Roll out the pastry into a rectangle measuring 19" x 15"/50cm x 40cm. Cut the pastry in half long ways so that you have two long, narrow pieces of pastry.

On one piece of pastry, imagine it divided into four and dollop the filling evenly in the centre of each section.

Brush some beaten egg over the pastry edges. Place the other piece of pastry over the top and press down around the edges and between the filling. Brush the top piece of pastry with the remaining beaten egg. Slice into four.

Spread out on a baking sheet and bake for about 20 minutes until puffed up and golden. Serve hot or cold.

SARDINE PÂTÉ

Vegetarian

No cooking

Serves 2

Preparation 5 minutes

Light, refreshing flavours using a can of sardines.

4oz/120g can sardines drained
1 small or ½ large lemon
4 heaped tbsp natural, unsweetened yogurt (Greek is ideal)
½ cucumber
2 tbsp parsley (or herb of your choice e.g. basil)
Small bunch chives
Black pepper

Put the sardines in a bowl and break up with a fork.

Squeeze the juice from the lemon over the sardines. Add the yogurt. Chop the cucumber finely and add to the bowl. Chop the herbs and add them to the bowl together with black pepper to taste. Mix well.

Serve with vegetable sticks or breadsticks, melba toast etc.

NOTES

THANK YOU

Thank you for reading my book! I do hope you enjoyed making the recipes.

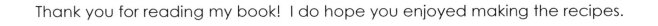

http://www.thriftycook.co.uk

Printed in Great Britain
by Amazon

81626731R00027